Spannender Kontrast: Die neue Treppe im historischen Kern der Stadt.
Fascinating contrast: new stairway in the historic city centre.

Iserlohn

... immer sympathischer
... an Endearing City

Mit Texten von Hildegard Goor-Schotten
und Fotos von Klaus Schlünder

With texts by Hildegard Goor-Schotten
and photographs by Klaus Schlünder

Verlag Beleke

Der Danzturm, 1908/09 an der ehemaligen Telegrafenstation auf dem Fröndenberg errichtet, ist das markante Wahrzeichen der Stadt.

The Danzturm is a distinctive landmark of the city. It was built in 1908/9 on the site of the former telegraph station, located on the Fröndenberg.

Inhalt

Contents

Herausgeber: Norbert Beleke

Text und Konzeption: Hildegard Goor-Schotten
Fotos: Klaus Schlünder, Stadt Iserlohn
Hans Blossey: Vorsatz, S. 2, 8-9, 11, 56, 66 o., Nachsatz
Märk. Arbeitgeberverband: S. 61 · Privatbrauerei Iserlohn: S. 63 (2)
THIELE: S. 64 (2) · KIRCHHOFF Gruppe: S. 65 (2) · Weyland: S. 66 u. (2)
BiTS: S. 70 u., 71 m.r. · NASA/Walter: S. 71 u.
Sudhaus: S. 60 o. · Medice: S.60 u.
Sauerland-Tourismus e. V.: S. 73; S. 76 (2), u.r. Ralph Lueger; S. 77, u. Klaus Deiter;
S.79 (3), u.r. Jürgen Fischbach, u.l. Ralph Lueger;
LGS Hemer/Tölle: S. 80

Wir danken dem Presseamt der Stadt Iserlohn für die freundliche
Unterstützung und Begleitung dieses Buches.

Übersetzung: St. Clair Consulting
Lektorat und Projektleitung: Thomas Sliepen
Gesamtherstellung: Verlagsgruppe Beleke
Grafische Gestaltung: Jürgen Mosler

Verlagsgruppe: Verlag Beleke, Essen, Aachen, Dortmund, Lübeck, Wiesbaden
NOBEL-Verlag GmbH, Essen – DAS RATHAUS Verlagsges. mbH, Essen
SCHMIDT-RÖMHILD - Deutschlands ältestes Verlags- und Druckhaus seit 1579 -
Lübeck, Berlin, Essen, Wiesbaden
HANSISCHES VERLAGSKONTOR GmbH, Lübeck
SCHMIDT-RÖMHILD Verlagsgesellschaft mbH Leipzig, Rostock, Schwerin
Wendler-Verlag, Aachen
ELVIKOM Film-Verlag GmbH, Essen
ntv neue television FILM-TV-PRODUKTION GmbH, Essen
www.beleke.de

ISBN 978-3-8215-0619-7

Das Grün dominiert beim Blick über die Stadt.

The city of Iserlohn is dominated by park- and woodland.

Zentrum in und für die Region

I*iiserlohn* – wird der Ortsname so ausgesprochen – und Außenstehende machen dies oft und gerne – zuckt der Einheimische zusammen. Die dritte Silbe wird betont – das werden die Waldstädter, durchaus ein wenig stur, nicht müde zu erklären. Vielleicht liegt es daran, dass dieses „lohn" der Kern der von ihnen oft ein wenig herunter geputzten, aber eigentlich doch geliebten Heimatstadt ist?

„Lon", althochdeutsch für Wald, taucht in den Schriften erstmals um 1150 als Bezeichnung für die kleine Ansiedlung auf einer vom Baarbach umflossenen Insel auf. Erst später kam das „iser" dazu: Eisen. Metall und Wald – das sind die beiden Elemente, die die Stadt bis heute am meisten geprägt haben.

Ihre Geburtsstunde liegt im Dunkeln. Die Pankratiuskirche, das älteste Gebäude der Stadt, stammt aus dem 9. Jahrhundert und war Zentrum der ursprünglichen Siedlung. 1278 bestätigte Graf Eberhard I. von der Mark die Stadtrechte. Da wird es aber schon die befestigte Ansiedlung auf dem Bilstein gegeben haben, hoch über der „Bauernkirche", die geistlicher Mittelpunkt der Landbevölkerung in der Umgebung war. Die Stadt entwickelte sich dort oben, rund um die 1350 ausgebaute Oberste Stadtkirche. In den folgenden Jahrhunderten wuchs sie vor allem Richtung Norden und Nordosten – und wurde immer wieder durch Brände teilweise fast komplett zerstört. Auch beim letzten großen Stadtbrand 1712 blieben nur 47 von 460 Häusern stehen.

In der Rückschau kann dies auch als Fanal betrachtet werden.In den folgenden zwei Jahrhunderten entwickelte sich die Stadt rasant. Drahtherstellung und Galmeibergbau, schon damals

Centre in and for the region

Whenever the town's name is pronounced as *"Iiserlohn"* – something which outsiders often do – locals cringe. Somewhat stubborn, they never tire of explaining that the emphasis falls on the third syllable. Perhaps it's because "lohn" represents the heart of this town. Because although locals may often find fault with their home town, there is no doubt that they are also very fond of it.

"Lon" – old German for "forest" – is first mentioned in records dating from around 1150 as the name of a small settlement on an island surrounded by the River Baarbach. "Iser" was added later as an allusion to iron. Metal and trees – those are the two elements which have had the greatest effect on the town to date.

No one knows when the town was first established. Pankratiuskirche – the town's oldest building – dates from the 9th century and formed the centre of the original settlement. In 1278, Count Eberhard I von der Mark approved the town charter. By then, the fortified settlement on Bilstein already existed, high up above the Bauernkirche, which formed the focal point of religious life for the local rural population. The town developed on the hill around the Oberste Stadtkirche, which was extended in around 1350. Over the following centuries, the majority of the town's growth was in the north and north-east, although a series of fires repeatedly caused widespread damage. In 1712, the last major fire wiped out all but 47 of the town's 460 houses.

With hindsight, this can be viewed as a turning point. The town developed rapidly over the following two centuries. Wire manufacturing and calamine mining – well-established industries even back then – laid the foundations for

Iserlohn um 1830.

Iserlohn (around 1830).

traditionsreiche Gewerbezweige, legten den Grundstein für einen wirtschaftlichen Aufschwung. Arbeiterwohnungen, Fabriken, aber auch prachtvolle Villen der Unternehmer und Kaufleute entstanden vor den Toren der Stadt.

Gelitten hat dabei der Wald. Kahl waren die Hügel rund um Iserlohn, als ein unbekannter Künstler die Stadt um 1830 in zarten Farben auf die Leinwand bannte. Die intensive Beweidung durch Ziegen, den „Kühen der Bergleute", und vor allem der immense Bedarf an Brennmaterial hatten die Wälder im 18. Jahrhundert auf ein Minimum schrumpfen lassen. Die Stadt und vor allem der Verschönerungsverein, untrennbar verbunden mit dem Namen des Lehrers Ernst Danz, kümmerten sich in der zweiten Hälfte des 19. Jahrhunderts um die Aufforstung und die Anlage von Spazierwegen. Iserlohn wurde wieder zur Waldstadt.

Das ist sie, trotz der großen Schäden durch den Orkan Kyrill im Jahr 2007, noch immer. Fast überall hat man das Grün vor Augen. Rund 4500 Hektar der 12550 Hektar Gesamtfläche sind Wald, weitere 4500 Hektar werden landwirtschaftlich oder gärtnerisch genutzt. Die attraktiven Naherholungsgebiete direkt vor der Haustür – das zeichnet Iserlohn nach wie vor aus.

Völlig verändert hat sich seit den 1960er Jahren dagegen das Bild der Innenstadt. Von Kriegsschäden weitgehend verschont geblieben, machten die extrem verdichtete Bebauung, die engen, verwinkelten Straßen und die schlechte Bausubstanz eine Sanierung unumgänglich. Die eingeleiteten Maßnahmen ließen ganze Straßenzüge zugunsten des ausgebauten Innenstadtringes, zentraler Plätze und moderner Gebäude verschwinden. Das Ergebnis überzeugte nicht in je-

an economic upturn. Workers' housing and factories sprung up outside the town along with magnificent villas for the merchants and industrialists.

All of this was achieved at the expense of the forest. When an unknown artist painted Iserlohn in delicate colours on his canvas in around 1830, the hills surrounding the town were bare. Intensive grazing by goats and above all the immense demand for fuel dramatically reduced the forests in the 18th century. In the second half of the 19th century, the town and especially the Improvement Association – which is inextricably linked with the name of the teacher Ernst Danz – dedicated themselves to restocking the forests and establishing hiking paths. Iserlohn regained its woods.

And even after the extensive damage caused by Hurricane Kyrill in 2007, Iserlohn remains a heavily wooded town. There is green almost everywhere you look. Some 4,500 of the 12,550 hectares covered by the town are forests and another 4,500 hectares are used for agriculture or gardens. Attractive recreational areas right on their doorsteps – an added bonus for the people of Iserlohn.

However, the town centre's face has changed completely since the 1960s. Largely spared in WWII, the extremely dense development, narrow, winding streets and poor building fabric made redevelopment essential. During the ensuing projects, whole streets disappeared to be replaced by the extended ring road, central squares and modern buildings. The results were not always well received. Many people are keen to reverse some of the architectural faux-pas. A long-term project was initiated in the early 1990s

Das Glockenspiel an der Unnaer Straße, ein Geschenk Iserlohner Bürger, spielt viermal täglich – unter anderem das Westfalenlied, das Emil Rittershaus 1869 im Gasthaus schräg gegenüber dichtete.

The chimes on Unnaer Strasse, a gift presented by a group of Iserlohn citizens, can be admired four times a day. Among the musical repertoire is the so-called Westfalenlied, which Emil Rittershaus wrote in 1869 in the restaurant across the road.

dem Fall. Manche Bausünde möchte man wieder rückgängig machen. Begonnen hat man damit Anfang der 1990er Jahre, als ein langfristiges Projekt zur Attraktivitätssteigerung der City in Gang gesetzt wurde.

Aber auch Privatleute haben viel Engagement und Geld in den Erhalt alter Bausubstanz gesteckt. Das beste Beispiel ist die Schauburg, die von einer Unternehmerfamilie gekauft und wieder zu dem gemacht wurde, was sie einst war: ein glänzender Veranstaltungsort an einer markanten Stelle der Stadt.

Auch in vielen anderen Straßen sieht man sanierte historische Fassaden und Gebäude, die den Charme Iserlohns ausmachen und das moderne Erscheinungsbild der Fußgängerzone – bei ihrer Einweihung 1979 übrigens die erste in Südwestfalen – oder des Stadtbahnhofs ergänzen.

Durch den Abzug der britischen Truppen und der Bundeswehreinheiten nach 1990 musste auch an anderen Stellen in der Stadt gehandelt werden. Auf den ehemaligen Kasernengeländen entstanden ein attraktiver Wohnpark und ein neues Gewerbegebiet, siedelten sich eine private Hochschule und ein Internat sowie das Zentrum für Gerontotechnik an.

Iserlohn bleibt in Bewegung – die Veränderungen sind noch längst nicht abgeschlossen. Aber schon jetzt hat sich die Innenstadt wieder zu einem lebendigen Anziehungspunkt für viele Menschen auch aus dem Umland entwickelt, die hierher zum Einkaufen, Bummeln und Feiern kommen – ein Zentrum in der und für die Region, das in seinem Nebeneinander von Industrie und Natur viele schöne Seiten hat.

to address these and make the town centre more attractive.

Private homeowners have also poured a lot of commitment and money into maintaining the town's historic buildings. The best example is the Schauburg, which was bought by a family of industrialists and transformed back into what it once was: a stunning event venue in a prominent position within the town. Many other streets also boast restored historic facades and buildings which give Iserlohn its charm and complement the modern-looking pedestrian precinct – the first in south Westphalia when it opened in 1979 – and railway station.

Following the withdrawal of British and German troops, other parts of the town needed a facelift after 1990. The former barracks were replaced by attractive housing and a new industrial estate along with a private college, a boarding school and the centre for gerontechnology.

Iserlohn is still a work in progress – there are many more changes yet to come. But the town centre has already been transformed back into a lively magnet for many people from the surrounding area, who come here to shop, while away their free time or celebrate with friends. Iserlohn serves as a centre at the heart of the region. It is a town where industry and nature coexist side by side and a place which has plenty to offer.

Der Wochenmarkt auf dem Schillerplatz ist an jedem Mittwoch und Samstag Treffpunkt der Iserlohner.

The weekly market in Schillerplatz takes place every Wednesday and Saturday and has become a meeting place for the people of Iserlohn.

„Iserlohn,
– älteste und größte Stadt im Märkischen Kreis,
– frühindustrielles Zentrum, bekannt für Messing- und Bronzewaren, Drähte und sanitäre Armaturen,
– innovativer Standort neuer Technologien und der Recycling- und Entsorgungsindustrie, aufgeschlossen und modern,
– Stadt der Bildung, der Fort- und Weiterbildung und der kulturellen Vielfalt,
– Stadt mit hohem Freizeitwert und guten Einkaufsmöglichkeiten in Kaufhäusern und in gut sortierten Fachgeschäften,
– attraktiver Wohnort mit vielen Grünanlagen und Naherholungsgebieten, Sport- und Spielflächen.
Ein Bild sagt mehr als 1.000 Worte!
Das vorliegende Buch stellt die Stadt Iserlohn in ihrer ganzen Vielfalt vor. Genießen Sie interessante Blicke auf die ‚Waldstadt' und eine unterhaltsame Lektüre!"

"Iserlohn,
– the oldest and largest city in the Märkische Kreis district,
– an early industrial centre, renowned for its brass- and bronzeware, wire and bathroom fittings,
– a centre of innovation for new technologies as well as the recycling and waste management industry, visionary and modern in its approach,
– a city of education, academia and cultural diversity,
– a city with superb leisure attractions as well as excellent shopping facilities with a range of well-stocked department stores and specialty shops,
– an attractive place to live with an extensive green belt, hectares of forest and many sports and recreational facilities.
A picture says more than a thousand words.
This superb book showcases the City of Iserlohn in all its splendid diversity. I hope you enjoy the many vistas of our 'Waldstadt' as well as the fascinating historical insights."

Dr. Peter Paul Ahrens, Bürgermeister · Mayor

Eng beieinander stehen Bauernkirche und Oberste Stadtkirche (Bildmitte) im Kern der Stadt.

Standing almost side by side, Bauernkirche and Oberste Stadtkirche (centre).

Das Herz der Stadt: Vom Fritz-Kühn-Platz führt eine großzügige Treppe zum Burgmannshaus direkt neben der Obersten Stadtkirche. Das älteste weltliche Gebäude Iserlohns war Lateinschule, Gefängnis, Kindergarten. Heute beherbergt es die wertvolle Varnhagensche Bibliothek.

In the very heart of the city: a generously designed flight of stairs leads from Fritz-Kühn-Platz to Burgmannshaus, situated next to Oberste Stadtkirche. The oldest secular building in Iserlohn has served as a Latin school, a prison and a kindergarten. Today it houses the precious historic book collection of the Varnhagensche Bibliothek.

BUS

Um den Erhalt der Bauernkirche, des ältesten Iserlohner Gebäudes, kümmert sich seit 2005 ein Förderverein.

Since 2005, the Bauernkirche, oldest building in Iserlohn, has been looked after by a Förderverein.

Das sogenannte Rampelmannsche Haus wurde 1748 gebaut – ein schönes Beispiel des schlichten Spätbarocks am Fritz-Kühn-Platz.

The so-called Rampelmannsche Haus was built in 1748; it is a perfect example of the unobtrusive style of the late baroque period found in Fritz-Kühn-Platz.

Das Städt. Seniorenzentrum dominiert den umgestalteten Bahnhofsvorplatz. Zur Grundsteinlegung des ehemaligen Hospitals 1853 kam auch der spätere Kaiser Wilhelm I.

The building of the Municipal Centre for Senior Citizens dominates the redesigned forecourt of the main railway station. In 1853 the foundation stone of the former hospital was laid in the presence of the Prince of Prussia, who was later to become Emperor William I.

Tor in die Stadt, Domizil der Volkshochschule, erster Wanderbahnhof Nordrhein-Westfalens: der neue Stadtbahnhof.

The new city railway station acts as gateway to the city; it houses the Volkshochschule and is the first station in North Rhine-Westphalia to offer special services for hikers.

Sehen und gesehen werden – das gilt bei der „Eroberung“ der Kunst vor der Post, für die schönen alten Villen rechts und links der Baarstraße oder beim Eis essen auf dem Neuen Marktplatz.

To see and to be seen is the motto when admiring the art display outside the post office and the beautiful old mansions to the left and the right of Baarstrasse, or when enjoying an ice cream in Neuer Marktplatz.

Einen Platz in der Sonne bietet die Stadt im Sommer für alle Geschmäcker: beim „ersten“ Konditor der Stadt, vor der sanierten Schauburg oder „mittendrin“ in der Fußgängerzone.

Iserlohn offers plenty of summer fun and caters to all tastes at the most popular café of the city, situated in front of the restored Schauburg cinema, right in the very heart of the pedestrian zone.

Nicht alles Alte fiel der Sanierung zum Opfer: Abseits der Hauptstraßen lässt sich noch manch malerischer Winkel entdecken.

Although restored, the city has kept some of its old charm: away from the main streets, there are a number of picturesque nooks and crannies.

Für die „neue“ Stadt gab es im Zuge der kommunalen Neuordnung 1975 am Schillerplatz auch ein Rathaus im Stil der Zeit.

In keeping with the times, a town hall was built in Schillerplatz in 1975 for the “new” city.

Seit mehr als 100 Jahren bringt der Wochenmarkt Farbe auf den Schillerplatz.

The weekly market has been adding colour to Schillerplatz for more than a hundred years.

Der Renner im Sommer bei den Kindern ist das Wasserspiel vor dem Alten Rathaus.

The fountains in front of the old town hall are a great favourite with children during hot summer days.

Apotheken-Gebäude und Altes Rathaus aus den 1850er- bis 1870er Jahren prägen den modernen Platz im Zentrum der Stadt.

A pharmacy and the Altes Rathaus dating back between the 1850s and the 1870s respectively dominate the modern square in the city centre.

Großzügig und hell: Die erste Fußgängerzone Südwestfalens lädt nach ihrer Umgestaltung zum entspannten Bummeln ein.

Spacious and light: the first pedestrian zone in Southern Westphalia is perfect for a leisurely stroll, particularly now that is has been revamped.

Beim Bummel durch die Stadt lohnt sich ein Blick nach oben. Viele historische Fassaden sind aufwändig renoviert worden und überraschen mit manchem oft übersehenen Detail.

Many of the old façades with their intricately designed details have been painstakingly restored and are well worth a second glance.

Kommst Du
Freund dann
Die Tuer soll
DIR
sein

Wegen ihrer Nacktheit nicht unumstritten hat Skulptur „Elena“, Geschenk einer Bürgerin, ein behütetes Plätzchen an der Seniorenwohnanlage „Altes Stadtbad“ erhalten.

Quite a controversial nude – "Elena", the gift of an Iserlohn citizen, has been given a quiet space near the "Altes Stadtbad", home for senior citizens.

Alte und neue Architektur, durch den Torbogen vom Nolten aus gesehen.

Old and contemporary architecture, as seen through the gate from Nolten.

Nach der jüngsten Sanierung präsentiert sich die Jugendstilfassade von B&U wieder fast so wie zu den Gründungszeiten des Kaufhauses.

After painstaking renovation, the Art Nouveau façade of B&U shines in new splendour – a journey back in time to the period when the department store first opened.

Im alten Hauptpostamt, 1882 bis 1886 gebaut, sind heute Stadtarchiv und Verbraucherzentrale zu finden.

The old main post office, built in 1882 to 1886, today houses the city archives and the consumer advice centre.

Der Danzturm mit Restaurant und Aussichtsplattform ist ein beliebtes Ausflugsziel mitten im Wald.

The Danzturm is surrounded by woods. With its restaurant and an observation platform, it is a popular destination for outings.

Das weithin sichtbare Wahrzeichen Iserlohns thront seit 1909 hoch über der Stadt auf 384,5 m ü NN.

In 1909, the landmark of Iserlohn was built high above the city, at 384.5 metres above sea level.

Die Fassade und der Turm der Seniorenwohnanlage „Altes Stadtbad" erinnern an das prächtige Jugendstilbad, das bis 1986 hier am Poth stand.

The façade and the tower of the "Altes Stadtbad" home for senior citizens is indicative of the magnificent baths built in the Art Nouveau style, which dominated the location Am Poth until 1986.

Fachwerkidylle in der Historischen Fabrikanlage Maste-Barendorf.

Historic factory buildings of Maste-Barendorf with half-timbered architecture.

Erinnerungen an die industrielle Vergangenheit des heutigen Museums- und Künstlerdorfes.

Museums- und Künstlerdorf – reminders of an industrial past.

Das Pendant zum Danzturm im Seilerwald: Der Bismarckturm ist 338 Meter über dem Meeresspiegel gelegen.

Counterpart to the Danzturm in Seilerwald: the Bismarckturm, built 338 metres above sea level.

Der Seilersee, 1914 als Talsperre angelegt, ist zu jeder Jahreszeit reizvoll und ein beliebtes Ausflugsziel, das mit einer Fülle an Freizeitmöglichkeiten aufwartet.

The Seilersee dam was built in 1914 and is a charming and popular destination throughout the year. It offers a wide range of leisure activities.

Winterpause für die Tretboote am Seilersee.

Winter break for pedaloes on Seilersee.

Schneeidylle im Stadtwald.

Winter wonderland in the Stadtwald park.

Der Hang unterhalb des Danzturms ist in schneereichen Wintern Treffpunkt vieler Wintersportfans.

The slope below the Danzturm is a perfect meeting place for winter sports enthusiasts.

Auch im Winter ein Hingucker: Die Betonfiguren der gebürtigen Iserlohnerin Christel Lechner auf dem Marktplatz.

A real eye-catcher even in winter: the concrete sculptures in Marktplatz, created by Iserlohn's own Christel Lechner.

Nicht nur im Winter ein Schmuckstück ist der wiederhergestellte Treppenaufgang von der Treppenstraße zum Bahnhofsvorplatz.

The restored stairway from Treppenstrasse to the main railway station forecourt is an architectural jewel.

An der Südstraße, hinauf zur Alexanderhöhe, ist manch prächtige alte Villa zu entdecken.

Many grand mansions can be seen along Südstrasse, leading up to Alexanderhöhe.

Letmathe – Zweiter Stadtkern im Westen

Rund 97 500 Menschen leben in Iserlohn. Damit ist die Waldstadt die größte Stadt im Märkischen Kreis, und das seit 1975.

Im Rahmen der kommunalen Neuordnung wurde sie damals mit den Gemeinden Letmathe, Hennen, Kalthof, Sümmern und Kesbern zusammengeschlossen.

27 000 Menschen wohnen heute im Ortsteil Letmathe mit den dazugehörenden Dörfern. Die "kleine Schwester" Iserlohns brachte neben einer jetzt fast 1000-jährigen Geschichte einiges mit in die neue Stadt: einen zweiten Stadtkern mit zentraler Geschäftsstraße, den alten Herrensitz Haus Letmathe, die St. Kilianskirche, wegen ihres imposanten Baus auch Lennedom genannt, die Dechenhöhle, den Volksgarten als grüne Oase am Rand des Stadtkerns und viele aktive und engagierte Menschen in Vereinen und Wirtschaft, die zahlreiche Aktionen und Feste auf die Beine stellen.

Letmathe – a second town centre to the west

Iserlohn is home to some 97,500 people, making the heavily wooded town the largest in the district of Märkischer Kreis.

This has been the case since 1975, when a municipal reorganisation saw it merge with Letmathe, Hennen, Kalthof, Sümmern and Kesbern.

27,000 people now live in Letmathe and its surrounding villages. Iserlohn's "little sister" has been in existence for almost 1,000 years and has enhanced the newly created town in several ways. The merger provided a second town centre and high street to the west, the historic manor *Haus Letmathe*, *St Kilianskirche* – also known as Lennedom due to its impressive construction – the *Dechenhöhle* stalactite cave, the *Volksgarten* park which provides a green oasis on the edge of the town centre, and plenty of active and dedicated people in clubs and businesses who work tirelessly to organise special events and festivals.

Beim Blick von oben zeigt sich: Auch Letmathe ist Waldstadt.

The bird's-eye-view shows that Letmathe is also a town surrounded by woods.

Im Alten Rathaus von Letmathe, 1903/04 an der Hagener Straße gebaut, ist heute die Polizeistation untergebracht.

The old town hall of Letmathe, built in 1903/04 on Hagener Strasse, has become home to the police station.

Auch in Letmathe lohnt sich der Blick nach oben auf die alten Fassaden.

Letmathe also offers many old façades – well worth a second glance.

Im alten Herrensitz Haus Letmathe, mittlerweile aufwändig saniert, ist die Stadtbibliothek und ein Heimatmuseum untergebracht.

The old Haus Letmathe manor has been painstakingly restored and houses the public library and a museum of local history.

Die katholische Pfarrkiche St.Kilian wird wegen ihres imposanten Baus auch Lennedom genannt. Wer die Gelegenheit hat, die 164 Stufen im Turm zu erklimmen, wird mit einem fantastischen Ausblick belohnt.

Because of its imposing structure, the Catholic parish church St. Kilian is often referred to as Lennedom. The tower with its 164 steps offers a breathtaking view of the surrounding landscape.

Die Brückenzöllner an der Bahnhofstraße erinnern an die Zeit, als für das Passieren der Bahnhofsbrücke bezahlt werden musste.

The Turnpike Keeper on Bahnhofstrasse is symbolic of the period when bridge toll had to be paid before crossing the Bahnhofsbrücke.

Der Markt war immer auch Handelsplatz für die neuesten Neuigkeiten – die „Marktfrauen“ an der Hagener Straße zeigen es.

The market has always been a popular place to catch up on the latest news and gossip; perfect example: market women on Hagener Strasse.

Bis in die 1930er Jahre reicht die Geschichte des Volksgartens zurück: eine grüne Oase und Schauplatz zahlreicher Veranstaltungen.

The history of the Volksgarten dates back to the 1930s – a green oasis and location for many interesting events.

Die städtische Musikschule, stilvoll untergebracht in einer ehemaligen Fabrikantenvilla an der Gartenstraße, ist aus dem kulturellen Leben der Stadt nicht wegzudenken.	*The municipal music school has found a splendid home in the former mansion of a factory owner, situated in Gartenstrasse. The school plays a very important part in the cultural life of the city.*

Zahlreiche Skulpturen sind im Straßenbild der Stadt zu finden. Die Brückenzöllner in Letmathe schuf der Bildhauer Gordon Brown.

The streets of the city showcase a number of interesting sculptures. The Turnpike Keeper in Letmathe was created by Gordon Brown.

Kultur pur

Wald, Industrie – ist da Platz für Kunst, Musik, Museen? Eindrucksvoll zeigt sich in Iserlohn, wie all diese Aspekte miteinander verbunden werden können, sich sogar aufs Beste ergänzen.

Mit einer Vielzahl an Museen kann die Stadt aufwarten, und nicht selten ist das Museum selbst ein Stück Geschichte. Dort, wo die Wurzeln des Ortes liegen, steht heute in unmittelbarer Nachbarschaft zur Bauernkirche das Stadtmuseum. 1763 erbaut, rückte es als Zeughaus, als Waffenlager für die Landwehr, während der stürmischen Revolutionstage 1849 in den Mittelpunkt des Geschehens. Diese unruhige Zeit wird heute im Museum ebenso anschaulich dokumentiert wie die Vor- und Frühgeschichte, Handwerk und Industrie, Vereinswesen und städtisches Leben. Nur wenige Schritte weiter macht das Museum für Handwerk und Postgeschichte im ehemaligen Masteschen Fabrikhaus, einem prächtigen Fachwerkbau, mit der Geschichte des Iserlohner Handwerks und der für die Handelsbeziehungen so wichtigen Transportwege bekannt.

In eine alte Fabrikanlage eingebettet findet sich auch das einzige Nadelmuseum Deutschlands. Die Historische Fabrikanlage Maste-Barendorf ist vom Messingwalzwerk zu einem idyllischen Fleckchen geworden, in dem neben dem Museum Künstler ihre Ateliers haben, regelmäßig

Cultural highlights

In a town known for its forests and industry, is there still space for art, music and museums? Iserlohn offers impressive evidence of how all of these aspects can be combined and even work hand in hand with one another.

The town can boast a number of museums, many of which are historic buildings in their own right. The town museum marks the place where the original settlement stood, right by the Bauernkirche church. Erected in 1763, the building took centre stage during the turbulent revolution of 1849, when it served as an armoury and weapons store for the national guard. Today, the museum portrays this unsettled time just as vividly as prehistory, early history, crafts and industry, local clubs and societies, and town life. Just a few steps away, the craft and postal museum in the former Mastesches Fabrikhaus – a magnificent half-timbered building – informs visitors about Iserlohn's craft heritage and the transport routes which were so important for its trade relations.

Germany's only needle museum is tucked away in a former manufacturing complex. The Historische Fabrikanlage Maste-Barendorf has been transformed from a brass rolling mill into an idyllic spot. Alongside the museum, it houses artists' workshops, regular brass foundry demonstrations, and a whole host of cultural events.

Rocksommer in Barendorf – ein Open Air-Genuss nicht nur, wenn die „Local Heroes" Pee Wee Bluesgang spielen.

Rock summer in Barendorf is always an exciting open air event, featuring "local heroes" Pee Wee Bluesgang as well as other bands.

die Gelbgießerei vorgeführt wird und eine Vielzahl an Kulturveranstaltungen stattfindet.

Ein ganz anderer Wirtschaftszweig wird in der SASE lebendig, der Sammlung aus Städtereinigung und Entsorgung. Die Dauerausstellung „Meine Stadt soll sauber sein" erzählt anhand von mehr als 50 Müll- und Kehrwagen und vielen anderen Exponaten die Geschichte der Städtereinigung in den vergangenen 100 Jahren.

Historisch wird es auch noch einmal im Haus Letmathe, einer Burganlage aus dem 15. Jahrhundert. Das Heimatmuseum erzählt die Letmather Geschichte mit einem Schwerpunkt auf der Landwirtschaft. Im jüngst restaurierten Gewölbekeller ist ein ganz besonderer Veranstaltungsraum entstanden. Musik, Kabarett, Vorträge, Lesungen finden hier statt – eine Kombination, die auch an anderen Orten in Iserlohn bestens ankommt.

The SASE brings a very different industry to life with its collection dedicated to municipal cleaning and waste disposal. Its permanent exhibition "Keep my town clean" featuring more than 50 dustcarts and road sweepers plus many other exhibits tells the story of how municipal cleaning has developed over the past 100 years.

Another historical highlight is Haus Letmathe, a 15th century castle complex. The local history museum is dedicated to Letmathe and its agriculture in particular. A very special events room has been created in the recently restored vaulted cellar. Music, cabaret, talks and readings all take place here – a combination which is also well received in other venues in Iserlohn.

With its varied programme of shows and breathtaking decorations – especially at Christmas time – the Parktheater attracts visitors from the town and beyond. The Städtische Galerie, which is also

„Iserlohn, eine Stadt mit Ecken und Kanten, jahrhundertealter Geschichte, früh industrialisiert mit tiefgreifenden ökonomischen und sozialen Folgen, heute mehr oder minder mit nahezu allen zeitgenössischen kommunalen Problemen behaftet, wunderbar im Grünen gelegen, mit markanten architektonischen Zeugnissen vergangener Epochen, aber auch mit steinernen Monumenten einer falsch verstandenen Urbanität versehen, ist – zusammengefasst – äußerst facettenreich in ihrer Wahrnehmbarkeit.

Zu diesen Facetten zählt auch das kulturelle Angebot unserer Stadt an ihre Bürger und Gäste.

Ob städtische Kultureinrichtungen oder freie Kulturanbieter: Die Vielfalt und Güte ist enorm, trotz aller finanzieller Einschränkungen.

In einer Zeit des Umbruchs wandeln sich ehemalige Gunstfaktoren und Leitbilder. Städte sind hiervon in besonderer Weise betroffen, da im Unternehmensbereich manche der früher dominierenden harten Standortfaktoren an Bedeutung verlieren und weiche Standortfaktoren eine zunehmende Wertschätzung erfahren. Aber auch als Lebensraum sind Städte verstärkt auf ein positives Image angewiesen. Die Vielfalt und Qualität des kulturellen Angebotes werden dabei mehr denn je zum imagebildenden Träger eines Stadtbildes. Darum gilt es, die kulturellen Stärken Iserlohns nicht nur zu erhalten, sondern zu stärken und weiter zu entwickeln."

"One way in which residents and visitors view our town is through the cultural activities on offer. From municipal cultural facilities to independent providers, the variety and quality is outstanding, despite all the financial restrictions.

In a time of upheaval, positive factors and ideals are being redefined. This affects towns in a specific way because some of the 'hard' factors which were once important for business locations are now losing importance and 'soft' factors are being valued more and more. In terms of housing, too, towns increasingly rely on cultivating a positive image. More than ever, the variety and quality of cultural services are becoming crucial to the way a town's image is perceived. That is why we not only need to maintain Iserlohn's cultural strengths but also consolidate and further develop them."

Gerd Schäfer M. A.
Leiter der städtischen Museen

Director of the town museum

Die Städtische Galerie hat im historischen Von Scheiblerschen-Haus mitten in der Stadt ein stilvolles Domizil gefunden.

The Städtische Galerie has found a stylish home in the historic Von Scheiblersches-Haus, located in the city centre.

Das Parktheater zieht mit seinem abwechslungsreichen Programm und der vor allem zur Weihnachtszeit atemberaubenden Dekoration die Besucher auch von auswärts an. Die Städtische Galerie – ebenfalls in einem geschichtsträchtigen Gebäude untergebracht – hat sich vor allem mit der Ausstellung bedeutender Fotografen einen Namen gemacht. Moderne Kunst findet in der Villa Wessel statt.

Musikalisch wird der Bogen ebenfalls weit gespannt, von den Rockkonzerten in Barendorf über den Jazzclub Henkelmann, hinter dem der Hot Club Iserlohn als ältester deutscher Jazzclub steht, bis zu den Herbsttagen für Musik und dem Internationalen Gitarren-Symposium, die weltweit bekannte Künstler nach Iserlohn ziehen.

Musik wird aber auch erfolgreich hausgemacht, in den städtischen und privaten Musikschulen oder in einem der zahlreichen, ganz unterschiedlich ausgerichteten Chöre. Die können immer wieder mit ihren Auftritten überzeugen – wie auch die Theatergruppen, allen voran das Schauspielensemble Iserlohn, die mit viel Leidenschaft und Können die Bretter, die die Welt bedeuten, erobern.

housed in a historic building, is particularly renowned for its exhibitions of work by major photographers. Modern art can be found at Villa Wessel.

The town also caters for a wide range of musical tastes, from rock concerts in Barendorf to the Henkelmann jazz club, which can trace its roots back to Germany's oldest jazz club, Hot Club Iserlohn. Then there is the autumn music festival and the International Guitar Symposium, which both attract globally renowned artists to Iserlohn.

There is plenty of home-grown musical talent too, both at the municipal and private music schools and in the town's many choirs, each of which has a very different focus. Their performances are always a pleasure – as are those of the local theatre groups, especially the Schauspielensemble Iserlohn, who tread the boards with passion and skill.

RWE
Umwelt
FAUN
1980-1990
FAUN
KRUPP

Post und Handwerk in der Region, Städtereinigung und Müllabfuhr gestern und heute, Höhlenbär und Dinosaurier: Die Museen und Sammlungen in Iserlohn und Letmathe machen die Besucher anschaulich und oft „begreifbar" mit den verschiedensten Aspekten der Vergangenheit bekannt.

Post offices and trade centres of the region, street cleaning and rubbish collection now and in the past, cave bears and dinosaurs: the museums and collections in Iserlohn and Letmathe offer visitors a fascinating insight into the rich history of this region.

In der Villa Wessel an der Gartenstraße lebte das bekannte Malerpaar Wilhelm Wessel und Irmgart Wessel-Zumloh.

The well-known artists Wilhelm Wessel and Irmgart Wessel-Zumloh live in a mansion in Gartenstrasse.

Das Parktheater auf der Alexanderhöhe ist mit seinem Programm und seiner Ausstattung zum kulturellen Anziehungspunkt in der Region geworden.

The Parkttheater on Alexanderhöhe, with its exciting setting and event programme, has become a cultural meeting place for the region.

Das Stadtmuseum präsentiert die Geschichte der Stadt – in einem Gebäude, das als ehemaliges Zeughaus selbst ein Stück Geschichte ist.

The Stadtmuseum outlines the history of the city of Iserlohn; it is housed in a building which was home to the former armoury.

In der Historischen Fabrikanlage Maste-Barendorf wird an die bedeutende Nadelindustrie erinnert.

The historic factory Maste-Barendorf shows examples of the once famous needle industry.

Das Museumsdorf ist aber auch Schauplatz für moderne Kunstausstellungen und Musikveranstaltungen.

The Museumsdorf also stages exhibitions of contemporary art and musical events.

Der Kunstverein Villa Wessel holt immer wieder bedeutende Kunstausstellungen nach Iserlohn.

The Kunstverein Villa Wessel invites renowned art exhibitions to Iserlohn on a regular basis.

Mit dem Schwerpunkt Fotografie ist die Städtische Galerie auch überregional bekannt geworden.

With its focus on photography, the Städtische Galerie has been able to make a name for itself even beyond the region.

Im Haus Letmathe wird vor allem die bäuerliche Kultur und Lebensweise der Region gezeigt.

Displays in Haus Letmathe are dominated by rural culture and the lifestyle of the region.

Kunstschmied Eduard Balbach hat an der Grüner Talstraße in Letmathe ein eigenes kleines Handwerkmuseum aufgebaut.

Ornamental blacksmith Eduard Balbach has established his own small crafts museum in Grüner Talstrasse in Letmathe.

Feiern in der einmaligen Atmosphäre Barendorfs ist vor allem im Sommer ein Genuss.

Feste feiern, wie sie fallen

Karneval in Iserlohn? Wer daran zweifelt, dass aus Westfalen echte Jecken werden können, sollte sich bei Gelegenheit in Hennen oder Sümmern unters närrische Volk mischen In den Iserlohner Karnevalshochburgen geht alljährlich die Post ab.

Doch auch ohne Pappnas' können die Iserlohner feiern, und das nicht zu knapp. Üppig gefüllt ist der jährliche Veranstaltungskalender. Genuss pur, Autosalon, Brücken- und Lichterfest in Letmathe, Rock in Barendorf, Come-together-Festival im Floriansdorf, Schützen- und Dorffeste rund um die Stadt und und und – an manchem Wochenende hat man die Qual der Wahl.

Besonders bunt wird es seit 2001 am Christopher Street Day, zu dem die Schwul-Lesbische Initiative im Märkischen Kreis einlädt. Ein Ausnahmezustand der anderen Art herrscht am ersten Juliwochenende. Zum Schützenfest des ältesten Vereins der Stadt, des Iserlohner Bürgerschützenvereins, zieht es auch viele ehemalige Waldstädter wieder in die Heimat. Als Familienfest etabliert hat sich mittlerweile das parallel stattfindende, 1991 als Anti-Schützenfest ins Leben gerufene Friedensfestival, das auf dem Fritz-Kühn-Platz „umsonst und draußen" Rockmusik und politische Inhalte transportiert.

Festivities in the unique atmosphere of Barendorf are a joyous occasion, particularly in the summer.

Plenty of reasons to celebrate

Carnival celebrations are an annual occurrence in many parts of Germany, especially the Rhineland. But what about in Iserlohn? Anyone who doubts that the people of Westphalia know how to stage a carnival should join the revellers in Hennen or Sümmern. Iserlohn's carnival strongholds will leave you in no doubt that the people here know how to let their hair down.

However, they don't need to don carnival costumes to get in the mood to party. There is no shortage of events throughout the year, including the gourmet festival Genuss pur, the Autosalon car show, entertainment and fireworks at the Brücken- und Lichterfest in Letmathe, Rock in Barendorf, the "Come together" Festival in Floriansdorf, various traditional shooting and village festivals in the local area, and plenty more besides. Locals are spoilt for choice on some weekends.

Since 2001, Christopher Street Day organised by the Märkischer Kreis district's gay and lesbian initiative has been a particularly colourful addition to the events calendar. The first weekend in July sees a major event of a different kind, when the town's oldest rifle club – Iserlohner Bürgerschützenverein – holds its traditional shooting

Was das Schützenfest für die Iserlohner, ist die Kiliankirmes zwei Wochen später für die Letmather. Seit mehr als 550 Jahren ist die alte Kirchweihkirmes ein Anziehungspunkt für Tausende von Besuchern auch von weiter her. Auf eine fast gleich lange Tradition als Kirchweihfest der früheren Bartholomäuskirche kann die Appeltatenkirmes in Oestrich blicken, auf der es nicht nur die leckeren Apfeltaschen gibt.

Etwas ganz Spezielles ist der Pfingstmontag. In aller Herrgottsfrühe pilgern die Menschen zum Ballotsbrunnen in den Stadtwald, um ein Glas Quellwasser zu trinken. Das verspricht, so die Sage, ein Jahr Gesundheit – das bunte Rahmenprogramm sorgt vor allem für Unterhaltung.

Zur Weihnachtszeit wird es dann besonders stimmungsvoll in der Waldstadt. Das Museumsdorf Barendorf bezaubert mit seinen alten Fachwerkhäusern und Kunsthandwerk. Im Park vom Haus Letmathe verbreiten ein vielfältiges Angebot und Programm Vorfreude auf das Weihnachtsfest. Und auch in der Iserlohner Innenstadt breitet sich mittlerweile wieder rund um Bauernkirche und Altem Rathaus weihnachtliche Stimmung aus.

festival, which also attracts many former residents back to the town. Established in 1991 as a pacifist alternative, the simultaneous Friedensfestival ("Peace Festival") has now also established itself as a family event. Staged in one of the town's squares (Fritz-Kühn-Platz), this free outdoors event features rock music and political messages.

Two weeks later, the people of Letmathe hold their main festival – the Kiliankirmes. This fair marks the consecration of the former Bartholomäuskirche and has been attracting thousands of visitors from near and far for more than 550 years. The Appeltatenkirmes in Oestrich has been in existence almost as long and boasts more than just the delicious apple turnovers that give it its name.

Whit Monday is a very special day in Iserlohn. At the crack of dawn, people make their way to the Ballotsbrunnen in the local forest to drink a glass of spring water. Legend has it that this will keep you healthy throughout the following year. A colourful programme of accompanying events provides plenty of entertainment.

The heavily wooded town is particularly atmospheric in the run-up to Christmas. The Museumsdorf Barendorf is a magical sight with its historic half-timbered buildings and craft workshops. A variety of events are held in the park at Haus Letmathe to get people into the Christmas spirit. The heart of Iserlohn surrounding the Bauernkirche and the Altes Rathaus is also transformed into an atmospheric winter wonderland during the festive period.

Das Schützenfest mit den großen Umzügen durch die Stadt gehört zu den Höhepunkten im Veranstaltungskalender und gilt als größtes Volksfest Südwestfalens.

The marksmen's festival, with its grand parades leading through the city, is a major highlight on the list of annual events. It is the largest folk festival in Southern Westphalia.

Weihnachtsmärkte im Barendorf, rund um Haus Letmathe und in der Iserlohner Innenstadt ziehen in jedem Jahr viele Besucher von auswärts an.

Each year, Christmas markets in Barendorf, in the grounds of Haus Letmathe and in the city centre of Iserlohn attract many visitors from the region.

Die Lenne und ihre Brücken stehen im Mittelpunkt des Brückenfestes in Letmathe.

The river Lenne and its bridges are the focal point of the Festival of Bridges in Letmathe.

Das Naherholungsgebiet Seilersee (unten) hat sich zu einem Zentrum der Freizeitaktiviäten entwickelt. Hier finden sich neben weiteren Sportanlagen zwei der vier Iserlohner Bäder: das Freibad Schleddenhof (links oben) und das Seilerseebad (links) mit Sauna und Solebad.

The recreational area of Seilersee (below) has become the centre of leisure activities. Alongside several sports grounds, two of the four public baths of Iserlohn, Freibad Schleddendorf (above left) and the Seilerseebad (left) with sauna and salt water pool, are located here.

Die Ruhr im Norden der Stadt lädt zu ausgedehnten Spaziergängen, Rad- und Kanutouren ein.

The river Ruhr in the north of the city is the perfect location for long leisurely walks, as well as cycling and canoeing tours.

Ganz schön aktiv

„Sauerland, mein Herz schlägt für das Sauerland" – wenn das Lied der Gruppe Zoff ertönt und blau-weiße Fahnen und Schals geschwenkt werden, dann weiß eigentlich jeder: Es ist Eishockey-Zeit am Seilersee. Seit dem Jahr 2000 spielen die Roosters in der ersten Eishockeyliga, mal mehr, mal weniger erfolgreich, aber beständig. Turbulente Jahre machte das heimische Eishockey zuvor durch, das 1954 von kanadischen Soldaten ins benachbarte Deilinghofen gebracht wurde und 1971 nach Iserlohn umzog. Die Fans blieben treu – 3000 bis 4000 füllen den „Hexenkessel am Seilersee" regelmäßig zu den Heimspielen.

Die Roosters sind nicht der einzige Verein, mit dem Iserlohn sich sehen lassen kann. Lange Zeit im Schatten der Kufenflitzer stehend, aber eigentlich noch erfolgreicher sind die Kollegen auf den Rollen. Die Eis-und Rollsportgemeinschaft Iserlohn, kurz ERGI genannt, gründete sich 1965 und schaffte mit der Rollhockeymannschaft 1970 den Aufstieg in die erste Bundesliga. Sechs Meistertitel, sechs Vizemeistertitel, drei Pokalsiege – die Iserlohner gehören zu den besten Mannschaften Deutschlands wie die Samurai Iserlohn zur ersten Garde der Inline-Skaterhokkey-Liga zählen. Ein Aushängeschild sind unter anderem auch die Iserlohn Kangaroos, die seit

Good sports

When the fans start singing "Sauerland, my heart beats for the Sauerland" and waving their blue and white flags and scarves, everyone knows it's time for ice hockey in the arena by Seilersee lake. The Iserlohn Roosters have been playing in the first division of the ice hockey league since 2000. Although they have varying success, they are a constant presence in the first division. Local ice hockey encountered turbulent times ahead of this. It was introduced to neighbouring Deilinghofen by Canadian soldiers in 1954 and moved to Iserlohn in 1971. The fans stayed loyal through thick and thin. At home matches, 3,000 to 4,000 regularly pack out the Seilersee arena, which is affectionately referred to as "bedlam" due to the lively atmosphere.

The Roosters are not the only club which Iserlohn can be proud of. Although they were long overshadowed by their colleagues on the ice, the roller hockey team are even more successful. The town's ice sports and roller skating club – Eis-und Rollsportgemeinschaft Iserlohn or ERGI for short – was established in 1965 and rose to the first division of the German league with its roller hockey team in 1970. They have won the championship six times, have come second a further six times and have also won the cup three

Jahren in der zweiten Bundesliga und Regionalliga Basketball spielen.

Aber nicht nur für Zuschauer ist Iserlohn ein sportlich interessantes Pflaster, denn natürlich kann man all das selber ausprobieren, und dazu noch viel mehr. Mehr als 50 Sportarten vom Fußball bis zum Rhönradfahren, rund 140 Sportstätten vom Freibad bis zum Segelflugplatz sind im Angebot. Und auch ohne Verein wird es nicht langweilig. Rund um den Seilersee, entlang der Ruhr, im Naherholungsgebiet Dröschede, im Volksgarten oder unterm Danzturm – die Naherholungsgebiete sind nahe bei und bieten neben dem Raum für Aktivitäten Platz, um die Seele baumeln zu lassen. Mehr als 50 Kilometer Rad- und 200 Kilometer Wanderwege laden unter anderem dazu ein. Und im Winter geht es dann raus in den Schnee: auf die kleinen Rodelhügel überall im Stadtgebiet, den Hang mit Flutlicht am Danzturm oder auf Piste und Loipen in Kesbern.

Egal, ob Eiseskälte oder sommerliche Hitze: Um die 10 Grad sind es immer in der Dechenhöhle in Letmathe. In einer der schönsten Schauhöhlen Europas können die Besucher dort spektakuläre und wunderschöne Tropfsteingebilde bewundern, oft mit besonderen Führungen oder Musik verbunden. Zum Schauplatz verschiedenster Veranstaltungen ist mittlerweile auch das Floriansdorf geworden. Hinter der hübschen Kulisse mit den kleinen Gebäuden steckt eine einzigartige Einrichtung zur Brandschutzerziehung – auch das ein echtes Aushängeschild der Stadt.

Das Floriansdorf neben der Feuerwache ist ein außergewöhnliches Zentrum der Sicherheitserziehung – und Schauplatz vielfältigster Veranstaltungen vom Konzert bis zum Tiergottesdienst.

times, making the Iserlohn squad one of the best in Germany. Similarly, Samurai Iserlohn are among the top teams in the rollerblade hockey league. The Iserlohn Kangaroos are another real asset to the town; the basketball side has been playing in the second division of the national league and the regional league for many years.

But Iserlohn is not just interesting for passive sports enthusiasts. Of course, those who are interested can also try any of these sports – and many more – for themselves. The town offers more than 50 sports from football to wheel gymnastics and some 140 sports facilities from an outdoor swimming pool to a gliding field. There is plenty to do without joining a sports club too. With various recreational areas nearby – around the Seilersee, along the River Ruhr, in Dröschede, the Volksgarten park and the public space around the Danzturm – there is plenty of space for leisure activities or just relaxing. More than 50 kilometres of cycle routes and 200 kilometres of footpaths are an ideal place to start. And in winter, there are plenty of opportunities to enjoy the snow: on the little toboggan hills dotted throughout the area, the floodlit slope by the Danzturm or the pistes and cross-country ski runs in Kesbern.

Regardless of whether its ice-cold or boiling hot outside, the temperature is always roughly 10 °C in the Dechenhöhle in Letmathe. Here, at one of Europe's most stunning show caves, visitors can admire spectacular and beautiful stalactites and stalagmites, often combined with special tours or background music. Floriansdorf now also hosts a wide range of events. Hidden behind the pretty facade with its little buildings is a unique facility for teaching children and teenagers about fire safety – another real boon for the town.

Floriansdorf Iserlohn, located next to the fire station, is a centre for safety training and a venue for a variety of events, ranging from concerts to church services for animals.

Unter den erfolgreichen Sportmannschaften sind die Roosters weit über Iserlohn hinaus die Publikumslieblinge.
Die Spiele in der Eissporthalle am Seilersee sind bekannt wegen der Stimmung unter den Fans.

Of all the city's successful sports teams, the Roosters are the most popular; they are known far beyond the city of Iserlohn.
The games staged at the indoor ice rink on Seilersee are renowned for their fantastic atmosphere.

Radfahren, Rodeln, Segelfliegen, Minigolfspielen - für mehr als 50 Sportarten findet sich in Iserlohn das passende Plätzchen.

Cycling, tobogganing, gliding, miniature golfing – Iserlohn offers facilities for more than 50 different types of sport.

Die Dechenhöhle in Letmathe, 1868 beim Bau der Eisenbahnlinie entdeckt, gehört zu den schönsten Schauhöhlen Europas.

The Dechenhöhle in Letmathe was discovered in 1868, during the construction of a railway line. It is one of the most breathtaking show caves in Europe.

Die Faszination der Tropfsteingebilde wird oft noch durch besondere Führungen oder Konzerte verstärkt.

Special guided tours and concerts add to the fascination of the extraordinary shapes of the stalactites.

Hinter der prächtigen alten Fassade werden bei der Firma Sudhaus, seit dem 19. Jahrhundert bekannt für ihre Schlösser, Produkte von höchster Qualität entwickelt und produziert.

Behind the magnificent old façade, Sudhaus has been designing and producing high-quality locks since the 19th century.

Die Firma Medice gehört zu den führenden Arzneimittelherstellern Deutschlands. Das bekannteste Produkt: Meditonsin gegen Halsschmerzen.

Medice ranks among the leading pharmaceutical manufacturers in Germany. Their best-known product: Meditonsin for the relief of sore throats.

Made in Iserlohn

Es geht die Sage, dass der erste Iserlohner den lieben Gott sofort gefragt hat: „und wo ist mein Fabriksken?“ Die Industrie - und hier vor allem die metallverarbeitende - hat Iserlohn über Jahrhunderte geprägt. Von den Fabriksken aus, den Betriebsstätten mitten in der Stadt, oft im Hinterhof gelegen und anfangs nur aus einem Zimmer bestehend, wurden schon immer Waren in alle Welt geliefert. Kettenhemden aus Iserlohn waren schon vor dem 16. Jahrhundert ein Exportschlager. Zwischenzeitlich boomte die Tuch- und Bänderproduktion, der Galmeibergbau legte den Grundstein für die Herstellung hochwertiger Messing- und Bronzewaren wie der berühmten Tabaksdosen. Zu Beginn des 19. Jahrhunderts war die Stadt eine der bedeutendsten Industriemetropolen Westfalens, die märkische Region eines der weltweit größten Industriegebiete.

Von der damals führenden Nadelindustrie ist nur noch eine Fabrik übrig geblieben, die Öhr-Nadeln produziert. Viele mussten aufgeben, manche hat sich rechtzeitig umorientiert. Eines der ältesten Iserlohner Unternehmen, die Kirchhoff-Gruppe, begann vor 225 Jahren als Nadelfabrik Stephan Witte und beschäftigt heute als bedeutender Zulieferer für die Automobilindustrie mehr als 5300 Mitarbeiter weltweit. Es ist dabei nur eines von vielen Iserlohner Unternehmen mit internationalem Ruf. Die Metallverarbeitung mit dem über Jahrhunderte gewachsenen Know-

Made in Iserlohn

The saying goes that the first man God created for Iserlohn asked: “So where's my workshop?” Industry, especially metalworking, has shaped Iserlohn for hundreds of years. Goods have always been produced in workshops (known as Fabriksken) in the heart of the town – often located in backyards and originally consisting of a single room – and then sold around the world. Chainmail made in Iserlohn was an export hit way back before the 16th century. Later, cloth and ribbon manufacturing boomed, then calamine mining laid the foundations for the production of high-grade brass and bronze goods such as the famous tobacco tins. In the early 19th century, the town was one of the most important industrial centres in Westphalia; the district of the Märkischer Kreis was one of the world's largest industrial areas.

Just one factory remains from what was once a leading sewing-needle industry. Many others had to close down, while some realigned their businesses in time. One of Iserlohn's oldest companies, the Kirchhoff Group, started out 225 years ago as the needle factory Nadelfabrik Stephan Witte and now employs more than 5,300 people around the world as a major supplier to the automotive industry. This is just one of many Iserlohn-based firms that have achieved international standing. Most of them still belong to the town's centuries-old tradition of metalworking.

„Als Unternehmer lebe und arbeite ich gern in Iserlohn, weil sich die Stadt als Wirtschaftsstandort für mittelständische Produktions-, Handwerks- und Dienstleistungsunternehmen ständig weiterentwickelt und die hierfür wichtigen Standortfaktoren pflegt. Dazu gehören beispielsweise die Verkehrsanbindung, hervorragende Aus- und Weiterbildungsmöglichkeiten und ein abwechslungsreiches Kulturangebot. So bietet das Parktheater Iserlohn neben einem attraktiven Bühnenprogramm das stilvolle Ambiente für gesellschaftliche Veranstaltungen. Ganz besonders schätze ich auch die Menschen, die Bodenständigkeit und Zuverlässigkeit mit Aufgeschlossenheit verbinden.“

“I like living and working in Iserlohn as a business owner. The town is constantly developing as a business hub for small and medium-sized production, skilled-trade and service companies and ensures that it has the necessary infrastructure. This includes transport links, outstanding opportunities for training and continuing professional development, as well as a varied range of cultural events. For example, the Parktheater Iserlohn offers both an attractive selection of shows and a stylish setting for corporate events. I am also very fond of the people, who are down to earth, reliable and open.”

Horst-Werner Maier-Hunke
Geschäftsführer DURABLE Hunke & Jochheim GmbH & Co. KG, Iserlohn
Vorsitzender des Märkischen Arbeitgeberverbandes

Managing Director of DURABLE Hunke & Jochheim GmbH & Co. KG, Iserlohn
Chairman of the Märkische employers' association

how macht immer noch den größten Anteil aus. Doch auch in der Kunststoff- und Pharmaindustrie, im Büroartikelbedarf oder der Entsorgungs- und Recyclingbranche können sich mittelständische Unternehmen aus Iserlohn an der Spitze behaupten. Daneben gibt es noch die echten Spezialitäten: Das Iserlohner Pilsener wird seit 1899 im Grüner Tal gebraut und seit 1895 schätzen Kenner das Qualitätsprodukt der Senffabrik G. Thomas an der Friedrichstraße.

Die gehört noch zu den Fabriksken, von denen neben den „Großen" immer noch welche bestehen, auch wenn viele Unternehmen mittlerweile in die Industriegebiete außerhalb der Innenstadt gezogen sind. Um sie und die Gewerbe- und Existenzgründerzentren kümmert sich seit 1959 die Gesellschaft für Wirtschaftsförderung, die älteste Einrichtung dieser Art in NRW.

Um die13 000 von rund 30 000 Beschäftigten arbeiten in Iserlohn im produzierenden Gewerbe. Aber auch das Handwerk mit rund 900 Betrieben und der Handel- und Dienstleistungsbereich mit knapp 17 000 Beschäftigten untermauern den Ruf Iserlohns als Mittelzentrum in der Region.

But Iserlohn is also home to small and medium-sized enterprises in the plastic and pharmaceutical industries, the office supplies sector, and the waste disposal/recycling branch which are at the top of their game. They are joined by some specialist producers: Iserlohner Pilsener has been brewed in Grüner Tal since 1899, and gourmets have been enjoying the high-quality mustard produced by Senffabrik G. Thomas in Friedrichstraße since 1895.

The latter is one of the few small-scale workshops which survive alongside the giants, but many companies have now relocated to the industrial estates outside the town centre. A business support organisation, Gesellschaft für Wirtschaftsförderung, was established in 1959 to assist both existing companies and the local business and start-up centres. It is the oldest organisation of its kind in North Rhine-Westphalia.

Approximately 30,000 people work in Iserlohn. Some 13,000 of them are employed in the manufacturing industry. Around 900 businesses focus on skilled trades, while the retail/service sector has a workforce of almost 17,000. These figures underline Iserlohn's reputation as a commercial hub within the region.

Das ehemalige Brause-Gebäude – „Die beste Feder, lieber Sohn, ist die von Brause Iserlohn" – ist zum Dienstleistungszentrum mit Raum für Existenzgründer, Berufsinformationszentrum und Agentur für Arbeit geworden.

The former Brause factory site – "The best nibs are made by Brause in Iserlohn" – has become home to a service centre for budding entrepreneurs, as well as a job information centre and labour exchange.

1899 gründeten 27 Bürger die Brauerei Iserlohn AG. 2003 wurde sie kurz vor der Schließung von drei Kaufleuten übernommen und als Privatbrauerei weiter geführt.

In 1899, twenty-seven citizens founded Brauerei Iserlohn AG. Just before its closure in 2003, it was acquired by three businesspeople, who continue to run it as a private brewery.

Seit 1899 wird im Grüner Tal Iserlohner Pilsener gebraut.

Grüner Tal Iserlohner Pilsener beer has been brewed since 1899.

Zu den erfolgreichen mittelständischen Familienunternehmen gehören die Kettenwerke Thiele, die ihre Produkte – rund 5000 Artikel – in alle Welt liefern.

One of the city's most successful medium-sized family-run enterprises is Kettenwerke Thiele. The company exports more than 5,000 different products to countries around the globe.

Seit 1935 werden im Kalthofer Werk Ketten unter anderem für den Bergbau und die Schifffahrt produziert.

Kalthofer Werk has been producing chains for the mining and shipping industry since 1935.

„Iserlohn bietet den Menschen eine ausgezeichnete Lebensqualität. Die Schönheit der waldreichen Umgebung sucht ihresgleichen. Die Infrastruktur hat eine direkte Verkehrsanbindung an das Netz der Bundesautobahnen. Das umfangreiche Kulturprogramm spricht mit seiner Vielfalt alle Bevölkerungsgruppen an. Die Bildungseinrichtungen lassen mit der Fachhochschule Südwestfalen, der Privathochschule BiTS, den Gymnasien, Realschulen und Hauptschulen mit offenem Ganztagsbetrieb nichts zu wünschen übrig. Die Städtische Musikschule gehört zu den größten und erfolgreichsten des Landes. Auch die Sportvereine tragen zum guten Ruf der Stadt bei. Wir Unternehmer halten Iserlohn für einen idealen Wirtschaftsstandort und unterstützen die Bemühungen von Politik und Verwaltung nach besten Kräften."

"Iserlohn offers people an excellent standard of living. The heavily wooded surroundings are unrivalled in their beauty. The infrastructure is directly linked to the German motorway network. The extensive range of cultural services is varied enough to appeal to all sections of the population. The education facilities leave nothing to be desired with the University of Applied Sciences Südwestfalen, the private BiTS Business and Information Technology School and various all-day secondary schools which run extra-curricular activities in the afternoons. The municipal music school is one of the largest and most successful in the state of North Rhine-Westphalia. The sports clubs also help to enhance the town's good reputation. We businesspeople believe that Iserlohn is an ideal company location, and we support the efforts of policymakers and administrative bodies to the best of our ability."

Dr.-Ing. Jochen F. Kirchhoff
Vorsitzender des Gesellschafterkreises und des Beirats der KIRCHHOFF Gruppe
Chairman of the shareholder association and advisory board at the KIRCHHOFF Group

Blick auf das KIRCHHOFF Produktionswerk in Iserlohn-Sümmern, Industriegebiet Rombrock.

View of the KIRCHHOFF production site in Iserlohn-Sümmern, located in the industrial area of Rombrock.

Gebäude- und Landschaftsarchitektur machen das Verwaltungsgebäude des Umwelt- und Entsorgungsunternehmens Lobbe auf einem ehemaligen Kasernengelände zu etwas ganz Besonderem.

Architecture and landscape gardening add a special touch to the administrative building of the waste management service provider Lobbe, located on the former site of the army barracks.

Aus der glorreichen Zeit der Nadelindustrie ist die Firma Weyland als einzige Fabrikationsstätte für Öhrnadeln in Iserlohn übrig geblieben. Hier werden in fünfter Generation Nadeln aller Art gefertigt.

Weyland is the only needle manufacturer left in Iserlohn, which was once a hub of the needle industry. The factory has been producing eye needles for five generations.

Zukunftsweisende Studiengänge, eine enge Zusammenarbeit mit der Wirtschaft und eine Lage im Grünen bietet die Fachhochschule Südwestfalen rund 2000 Studenten am Standort Iserlohn.

Lebenslanges Lernen

Die Innovationskraft der heimischen Wirtschaft ist nicht zuletzt zurückzuführen auf eine enge Zusammenarbeit mit den Forschungs- und Bildungseinrichtungen in Iserlohn. Schon die Gründung der Ingenieurschule 1948 entsprach dem Wunsch der Metallindustrie nach qualifizierten Fachkräften. Aufgegangen ist sie in der Fachhochschule Südwestfalen mit weiteren Standorten in Hagen, Meschede und Soest. In Iserlohn studieren mehr als 1800 Studenten in den Fachbereichen Informatik, Naturwissenschaften und Maschinenbau. Angeschlossene Forschungsinstitute widmen sich der Entsorgungs- und Umwelttechnik und dem Korrosionsschutz. Die enge Kooperation mit Unternehmen zeigt sich aber auch in den praxisorientierten Studieninhalten und dem Angebot des Verbundstudiums, das parallel zur Berufstätigkeit möglich ist.

Schon im Namen kommt die enge Verbindung zur Wirtschaft bei der „BiTS – die Unternehmerhochschule" zum Ausdruck. Unternehmer Dietrich Walther gründete im Jahr 2000 die private

Embracing the future with tailor-made degree courses and displaying a strong commitment to industry dialogue, the University of Applied Sciences Südwestfalen Iserlohn has attracted some 2000 students to its Iserlohn campus.

Lifelong learning

The innovativeness of local businesses has a lot to do with their close collaboration with Iserlohn's research and education facilities. This link between business and education stretches right back to 1948, when an engineering school was established to provide well-trained specialist staff for the local metal industry. The original school later became part of the Fachhochschule Südwestfalen (University of Applied Sciences) with additional sites in Hagen, Meschede and Soest. Iserlohn is also home to more than 1,800 students pursuing courses in IT, science and mechanical engineering. The affiliated research institutes are dedicated to waste disposal, environmental technology and corrosion prevention. Close cooperation with businesses also takes the form of practically orientated curricula and the opportunity to study part time while working.

Another college with strong corporate ties is BiTS. The private Business and Information Technology School was established by entrepreneur Dietrich Walter in 2000 on the site of the former

Gutes Lernen fängt bei den Kleinen an: Viel Geld wurde in den Ausbau der Offenen Ganztagsgrundschulen, wie hier „Auf der Emst“, gesteckt.

Efficient learning has to be established as early as possible: a great deal of money has been invested in the extension of all-day primary schools, as illustrated by "Auf der Emst" school.

Das Berufsbildungszentrum der Kreishandwerkerschaft hat sich zum größten Bildungsträger im Märkischen Kreis entwickelt.

The vocational training centre of the association of craftspeople has become the largest educational provider in the region of Märkischer Kreis.

Das Theodor-Reuter-Berufskolleg am Karnacksweg, bereits 1852 gegründet, gehört zu den Bildungseinrichtungen, die für die Aus- und Weiterbildung qualifizierter Fachkräfte sorgen.

The Theodor-Reuter Business College in Karnacksweg was founded as early as 1852; it is one of the educational centres specialising in advanced vocational training for skilled personnel.

Business and Infomation Technology School auf dem Gelände des ehemaligen britischen Militärhospitals am Seilersee. Rund 1000 Studenten belegen die mittlerweile 14 Studiengänge aus den Bereichen Management, Wirtschaft oder Medien. Seit 2005 hat sich das von Studenten organisierte Campus Symposium zu einer hochkarätigen internationalen Wirtschaftskonferenz mit Referenten wie Bill Clinton, Kofi Anan und Al Gore entwickelt.

Aber auch unterhalb der Hochschulebene bietet Iserlohn jungen Menschen ein breites schulisches Angebot. Vom Berufskolleg des Märkischen Kreises mit mehr als 4000 Schülern über Alten- und Krankenpflegeschulen bis zum Berufsbildungszentrum der Kreishandwerkerschaft wird ein breites Spektrum an Berufsausbildungen abgedeckt, auf das das allgemeine Bildungsangebot mit allen Schulformen gut vorbereitet. Viel wurde in den vergangenen Jahren in den Ausbau der offenen Ganztagsschule investiert, um allen Kindern einen optimalen Start zu ermöglichen. Mit der VHS und ihren etwa 750 Veranstaltungen im Jahr sowie anderen privaten, kirchlichen und berufsständischen Einrichtungen ist auch das Weiterbildungsangebot breit und ermöglicht ein Lernen bis ins hohe Alter.

British military hospital. It now runs 14 courses in the fields of management, economics and media and has some 1,000 students. Since 2005, the campus symposium organised by students has developed into a top-notch international economic conference with speakers including Bill Clinton, Kofi Anan and Al Gore.

Iserlohn also has a wide range of schools for young people below higher education level. A whole host of vocational qualifications are offered, from the Märkischer Kreis district vocational college with over 4,000 students to schools for trainee nurses and carers, and the district vocational training centre for skilled trades. The foundations are laid by a good selection of secondary schools. In recent years, a great deal has been invested in expanding the all-day school model with extra-curricular activities in the afternoons (most schools in Germany finish at lunchtime) to give all children the best possible start in life. A variety of additional courses and continuing professional development is also available. The local adult education centre runs around 750 events a year and is complemented by private, church-run and professional facilities. With so much on offer, there is no reason not to keep learning to a ripe old age.

„Ich lebe bereits seit 1973 in Iserlohn, und mein Wirken fand zunächst in den vergangenen Jahrzehnten stets außerhalb Iserlohns statt. Erst durch meine Gründung der Hochschule **BiTS – Business and Information Technology gGmbh & CO. KG** habe ich festgestellt, welch große wirtschaftliche Attraktivität nicht nur die Stadt Iserlohn, sondern auch das ganze Umfeld hat, denn die vielen mittelständischen Unternehmen, die zu einem Teil auch Weltgeltung haben, waren mir gar nicht, trotz meines Lebens in den ersten Jahrzehnten in Iserlohn, so bewusst.

Heute sehe ich Iserlohn als eine interessante, aufgeschlossene Stadt mit vielen Aktivitäten und auch Attraktivitäten sowie einem großen Netz von Familien- und Inhaber geführten Unternehmen, die darum bemüht sind, sichere Arbeitsplätze zu schaffen.

Es macht Spaß, in Iserlohn zu leben."

"I have been living in Iserlohn since 1973, but I always used to work outside Iserlohn. I only realised what a business hub Iserlohn and the whole surrounding area is when I founded the college **BiTS – Business and Information Technology gGmbH & Co. KG**. Despite having lived in Iserlohn for so long, I wasn't aware of the many small and medium-sized enterprises here, some of which have international standing.

Now, I see Iserlohn as an interesting, open town with lots of activities and attractions and a large network of family and owner-run businesses which strive to create secure jobs.

Iserlohn is a great place to live."

Prof. Dr. h.c. Dr. h.c. Dietrich Walther
Unternehmer und Hochschulpräsident

Businessman and college president

Auf dem Gelände des ehemaligen Britischen Militärhospitals haben sich ein Internat und die private Business and Information Technology School, BiTS, angesiedelt: ein Campus am Seilersee.

A boarding school and the private Business and Information Technology School (BiTS) have established themselves on the site of the former British military hospital – a campus on Seilersee.

„Einmal Iserlohner, immer Iserlohner!

Da kann man machen was man will. Ich bin in meinem Leben 18 Mal umgezogen, lebte drei Jahre im Ausland, kenne nahezu jede Kultur in Europa und reiste 160 Mal um die Erde. Und da sitzt man dann irgendwo auf der Welt in einem Café und wird plötzlich in einem Dialekt angesprochen, bei dem man die Ohren spitzt: Das ist ein Iserlohner! Es geht einem das Herz auf, man lächelt sich an und fühlt sich gleich miteinander verbunden. So ist es halt: Einmal Iserlohner, immer Iserlohner!"

"Once an Iserlohner, always an Iserlohner!"

It doesn't matter what you do. I've moved 18 times, spent three years living abroad, am familiar with almost every culture in Europe and have travelled around the world 160 times. Yet you can be sitting in a café anywhere in the world and suddenly someone speaks to you in a familiar dialect: they're from Iserlohn! Your heart soars, you smile at one another and feel an instant connection. That's just the way it is: once an Iserlohner, always an Iserlohner!"

Univ.-Prof. Dr. rer. nat. Ulrich Walter
Diplom Physiker · D-2 Astronaut
Ordinarius für Raumfahrttechnik an der Technischen Elite-Universität München

University professor Dr. rer. nat. Ulrich Walter
Physicist · D-2 astronaut

*Die Umgebung Iserlohns ist dörflich-ländlich geprägt, sei es in Kesbern (oben) oder in Sümmern (rechts).
Bei ausgedehnten Wanderungen lassen sich viele idyllische Flecken entdecken.*

The region surrounding Iserlohn is dominated by a rural countryside that is particularly popular with hikers; places like Kesbern (above) and Sümmern (right) are perfect examples.

Von Iserlohn aus per Fernwanderweg ins Sauerland – mit den ausgebauten Waldrouten ist das kein Problem mehr.

Starting from Iserlohn, well-developed paths lead through the wooded hills of the Sauerland, offering perfect conditions for hikers.

Rund um Iserlohn/ Tor zum Sauerland

Einen ganz neuen Blick auf Iserlohn bekommt, wer einfach mal drumherum wandert. Ein eigener IS-Wanderweg führt rund um die Waldstadt: 62 Kilometer schöne Landschaft und die Begegnung mit den Ortsteilen draußen vor der Stadt.

Der südlichste Vorposten ist das Bergdorf Kesbern, eine Station auf dem ebenfalls abzuwandernden ehemaligen Drahthandelsweg nach Altena. Mit rund 450 Einwohnern ist es der kleinste Ort mit ländlich-dörflichem Charakter. Mit fast 494 Metern findet sich hier am Rüssenberg der höchste Punkt Iserlohns. Die exponierte Lage sorgt dafür, dass sich in Kesbern die Wintersportler tummeln. Aber auch im restlichen Jahr laden die zahlreichen Wanderwege und der Flugplatz Hegenscheid zum Aufenthalt im Freien ein.

Über den Wixberg geht es nach Lössel und Pillingsen mit schönen Ausblicken auf die Stadt und die sagenumwobene Felsformation Pater und Nonne. Jenseits der Lenne liegen Lasbeck und Stenglingsen, in Richtung Iserlohn reihen sich Oestrich, Dröschede und Dröscheder Feld anein-

The area surrounding Iserlohn/gateway to the Sauerland

To see Iserlohn in a whole new light, just put on your hiking boots. A special trail leads around the heavily wooded town, offering 62 kilometres of stunning scenery and a glimpse of the villages which belong to Iserlohn.

The town's southernmost outpost is Kesbern. This hillside village is located on the former wire trading route to Altena, which walkers can also retrace. With some 450 inhabitants, it is Iserlohn's smallest community, and it has retained its rural charm and village feel. The highest point in Iserlohn can also be found here on Rüssenberg hill, which stands almost 494 metres high. Its exposed position makes it popular for winter sports. With its many footpaths and Hegenscheid airfield, there is plenty for outdoor enthusiasts to do all year round.

Crossing Wixberg hill takes you to Lössel and Pillingsen with beautiful views of the town and the legendary rock formation Pater und Nonne. On the other side of the River Lenne are Lasbeck and Stenglingsen, while Oestrich, Dröschede and Dröscheder Feld are strung side by side out

Auf Gut Lenninghausen, nahe der Ruhr, lädt eine der kleinsten Privatbrennereien Westfalens, die Gutsbrennerei Bimberg, zum Probieren ein.

On the Lenninghausen estate, near the river Ruhr, one of the smallest private distilleries in Westphalia, Gutsbrennerei Bimberg, invites visitors to sample its products.

ander. Idyllisch mutet der historische Ortskern Oestrichs mit seinen alten Fachwerkhäusern an. Steinzeitliche Fundstellen lassen auf eine Besiedelung der Gegend schon vor über 40 000 Jahren schließen.

Schälk und Stübbeken sind die westlichsten Zipfel Iserlohns. Ganz in der Nähe bietet der Humpfertturm einen schönen Ausblick bis nach Schwerte und Dortmund.

Die nächsten Stationen sind Rheinermark und Rheinen, die mit Refflingsen, Leckingsen und

towards Iserlohn. The historic centre of Oestrich is an idyllic sight with its half-timbered houses. Artefacts from the Stone Age have been found in this area, indicating that settlements existed here more than 40,000 years ago.

Schälk and Stübbeken form the western tip of Iserlohn. The nearby Humpfertturm offers a stunning view as far as Schwerte and Dortmund.

The next stops are Rheinermark and Rheinen, which – together with Refflingsen, Leckingsen and Drüpplingsen – make up Hennen/Kalthof

Wenn es schneit, dann als erstes in Kesbern: Hier treffen sich im Winter Skifahrer und Rodler, kann man bei einem Spaziergang durch die verschneite Landschaft tief Luft holen.

Kesbern is always the first to be hit by snow: in winter it is an ideal place for skiing and tobogganing, as well as for refreshing walks through a winter wonderland.

Die evangelische Johanneskirche in Hennen aus dem 12. Jahrhundert ist mit ihrer romanischen Gewölbemalerei ein besonderer Schatz im Stadtgebiet.

The Protestant Johanneskirche in Hennen dates back to the 12th century. Its beautifully painted ceiling in the Romanesque style is much admired.

Drüpplingsen den Stadtteil Hennen/Kalthof mit insgesamt rund 10 000 Einwohnern ausmachen. Hier im Norden Iserlohns ist die Ruhr ganz nah, die zu Kanu- und Radtouren oder Spaziergängen einlädt sowie Angler und Camper anzieht. Aus dem Jahr 1150 datiert die erste Nennung Hennens. Die Johanneskirche, in dieser Zeit gebaut, gilt als besonderer Schatz im Stadtgebiet. Der Segelflugplatz Rheinermark, Hof Emde in Kalthof mit seinen Bauernmärkten, der Biolandhof Ohler Mühle am Ruhrtalradweg oder die Historische Kornbrennerei Bimberg auf Gut Lenninghausen in Drüpplingsen sind beliebte Ausflugsziele.

Im Kirschblütendorf Sümmern leben rund 7000 Menschen. Mit einem der größten Industriegebiete, seinem alten Ortskern mit dörflichem Charakter und Neubaugebieten am Rand ist es ein Ort der Gegensätze.

Diese Verbindung von Industrie und Natur ist es auch, die Iserlohn zur Nahtstelle zwischen Ruhrgebiet und Sauerland macht. Von hier, der größten Stadt des Sauerlands aus, kann sich der Besucher die „Welt der tausend Berge" erschließen. Ihre landschaftliche Schönheit machte die Region schon Ende des 19. Jahrhunderts zu einem beliebten Ausflugsziel für die Bewohner des Ruhrgebietes. Die Berge vor der Haustür – das ist gerade im Winter eine echte Attraktion für sie und vor allem auch die Niederländer.

Seit einigen Jahren setzt man im Sauerland aber auch verstärkt auf den Wandertourismus. Neue,

with a total population of approximately 10,000. Here, in the north of Iserlohn, the River Ruhr is not far away, attracting canoeists, cyclists, walkers, anglers and campers. The first record of Hennen dates back to 1150. Johanneskirche, built at this time, is considered one of the area's real gems. Popular attractions include Rheinermark gliding field, Hof Emde in Kalthof with its farmers' markets, the organic farm Ohler Mühle on the Ruhr valley cycle route and the historic Bimberg corn schnapps distillery on the Gut Lenninghausen estate in Drüpplingsen.

Sümmern is home to some 7,000 people and has a stunning display of cherry blossom in springtime. With one of the largest industrial estates, a historic centre with a real village feel, and new peripheral housing estates, it is packed with contrasts.

This combination of commerce and nature is also what makes Iserlohn an interface between the industrial Ruhr area and the rural Sauerland. Iserlohn is the largest town in the Sauerland and the ideal starting point for visitors to discover this region, known as the "place of a thousand hills". Its superb scenery made the region a popular getaway for inhabitants of the Ruhr area as far back as the late 19th century. Especially in winter, the hills draw many city dwellers and Dutch tourists in particular to the area.

For several years now, the Sauerland has also been working hard to attract walkers. New, attraktive Fernrouten wie die Sauerland-Waldroute, der Sauerland-Höhenflug oder der Rothaarsteig ergänzen das gut ausgebaute Wanderwegenetz. Sie beginnen in Iserlohn oder sind von hier aus gut zu erreichen – nicht umsonst steht in der Waldstadt der erste ausgezeichnete Wanderbahnhof Nordrhein-Westfalens. Mit der LenneRoute, dem Ruhrtalradweg oder der BikeArenaSauerland kommen Radfahrer auf ihre Kosten. 17 Talsperren sind zum Paradies für Ausflügler, Angler und Wassersportler geworden.

Mit einer Fülle an Sehenswürdigkeiten kann das Sauerland das ganze Jahr über aufwarten. Die Burg Altena mit der ersten Jugendherberge der Welt, industrielle Erlebnismuseen, malerische Altstädte, ehrwürdige Klosteranlagen, prächtige Schlösser laden zum Besuch ein. Die Karl-May-Festspiele in Elspe, Freizeitparks oder die Fahrt mit einer der Museumseisenbahnen bieten besondere Erlebnisse. In Iserlohn, dem Tor zum Sauerland, ist man ganz nah dran.

attractive long-distance routes such as the woodland Sauerland-Waldroute, the hilly Sauerland-Höhenflug and the Rothaarsteig complement the well-established network of paths. The routes either begin in Iserlohn or can be reached easily from the town – the railway station was the first in North Rhine-Westphalia to be named a walker-friendly station, and with good reason. Cyclists are also well catered for with the LenneRoute, the Ruhr valley cycle route and the BikeArenaSauerland. 17 dams have created perfect spots for day trippers, anglers and water sports enthusiasts alike.

The Sauerland boasts many attractions all year round. There is plenty to see – from Burg Altena with the world's first youth hostel to living industrial museums, and from picturesque historic towns and sacred abbeys to magnificent stately homes. For a day out to remember, try a dramatisation of one of Karl May's westerns at the festival in Elspe, visit one of the amusement parks or ride on a historic railway. In Iserlohn – the gateway to the Sauerland – all of this is close at hand.

Von Iserlohn aus lassen sich schöne Ausflüge ins Sauerland unternehmen, so zum einmaligen Waldskulpturenweg zwischen Bad Berleburg und Schmallenberg (links), in den Vergnügungspark Fort Fun (unten links) oder nach Winterberg mit seinem Schlittenhunderennen und vielen Sportangeboten im Winter (unten rechts).

Starting in Iserlohn, many exciting excursions can be made into the beautiful Sauerland: to the wood sculpture trail between Bad Berleburg and Schmallenberg (left), the theme park Fort Fun (bottom left), the sledge dog race in Winterberg, or the many winter sports areas (below right).

Nicht weit ist es bis zu den Burgen des Sauerlandes. Burg Altena hoch oben auf dem Berg hat auch die erste Jugendherberge der Welt und ein Drahtmuseum zu bieten.

Iserlohn is just a stone's throw from the castles of the Sauerland. Burg Altena, built high on a hill, became home to the world's first youth hostel and also houses a wire museum.

Wer rund um die Stadt wandert, durchs Grüner Tal, an den sagenumwobenen Felsen Pater und Nonne vorbei, Lasbeck oder Oestrich streift und die Ausblicke auf Berge und Wald genießt, versteht, warum Iserlohn sich auch als Tor zum Sauerland präsentiert.

Skirting the boundaries of the city, hiking through Grüner Tal, past the legendary Padre and Nun rocks and Lasbeck and Oestrich, taking in the magnificent views of mountains and woodlands, it becomes clear why Iserlohn is called the Gateway to the Sauerland.

„Land der tausend Seen“ wird das Sauerland auch genannt. Listersee (oben), Diemelsee (rechts), Möhnesee (unten) oder eine andere der insgesamt 17 Talsperren bieten ideale Bedingungen für Wassersportler und Spaziergänger.

The Sauerland is also referred to as the "Land of the Thousand Lakes" – Listersee (above), Diemelsee (right), Möhnesee (below) or one of the 17 reservoirs are perfect for water sports and enjoyable walks.

Die Landesgartenschau 2010 zog mehr als eine Million Menschen ins benachbarte Hemer. Der Park bleibt den Besuchern als Naherholungsgebiet erhalten, den weiten Blick vom Jübergturm inklusive.

The Landesgartenschau 2010 attracted more than a million people to the neighbouring town of Hemer. The park area is a lasting attraction for visitors from the region, with a view from the Jübergturm as an added bonus.